PARA CYCLING

ETHAN OLSON

childsworld.com

Published by The Child's World®
800-599-READ • www.childsworld.com

Copyright © 2024 by The Child's World®
All rights reserved. No part of this book may be reproduced or utilized in any form or by any means without written permission from the publisher.

Photography Credits
Photographs ©: Tim Goode/PA Wire/AP Images, cover, 1; Shutterstock Images, 2, 6, 9 (bottom left); A. Ricardo/Shutterstock Images, 3 (top), 5, 15; Hairul Nizam/Shutterstock Images, 3 (bottom), 11; Gaie Uchel/Shutterstock Images, 7, 9 (top left), 9 (top right), 12; Marcus Brandt/picture-alliance/dpa/AP Images, 9 (bottom right); Bryn Lennon/Getty Images Sport/Getty Images, 17; Scott Heavey/Getty Images Sport/Getty Images, 19; Mauro Ujetto/NurPhoto/AP Images, 21

ISBN Information
9781503885141 (Reinforced Library Binding)
9781503885738 (Portable Document Format)
9781503886377 (Online Multi-user eBook)
9781503887015 (Electronic Publication)

LCCN 2023937296

Printed in the United States of America

ABOUT THE AUTHOR
Ethan Olson is a writer from Minneapolis, Minnesota. He enjoys sports, and he has written multiple children's books.

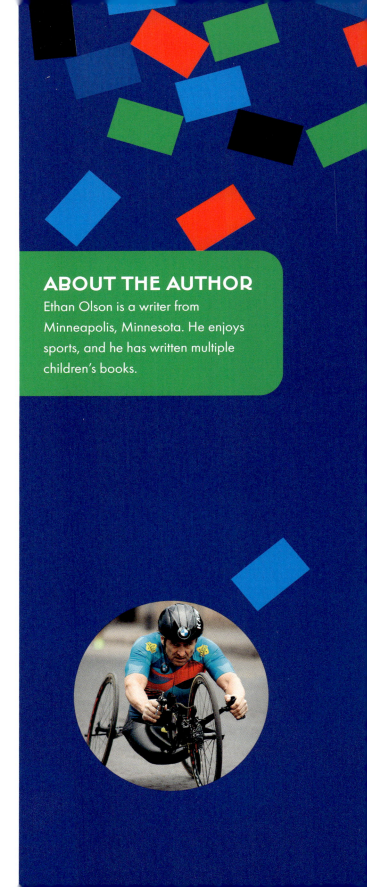

CONTENTS

CHAPTER ONE
PEDALING WITH PASSION . . . 4

CHAPTER TWO
CYCLING FOR ALL . . . 10

CHAPTER THREE
PARA CYCLING STARS . . . 16

Glossary . . . 22

Fast Facts . . . 23

One Stride Further . . . 23

Find Out More . . . 24

Index . . . 24

CHAPTER ONE

PEDALING WITH PASSION

As a buzzer sounded, Jacob drove his legs hard into his pedals. His bike steadily gained speed around the first curve of the track. Jacob was competing at the Para track cycling regional championships. He was the last athlete up in the 1-kilometer time trial event. Jacob's right leg had been **amputated** below the knee. The special **prosthetic** he used clipped into the bike pedal like any other racing shoe.

A 1-kilometer race consists of four laps. Jacob knew he had to save some energy for the end of the race. As he finished the first lap, Jacob grabbed the second set of handlebars higher on his bike. This helped him be more **aerodynamic**.

Jacob continued at a steady pace through the first three laps. The steep curves at each end of the track helped him maintain his speed. Jacob made sure to keep his bike on the inside part of the track. A race official rang a bell. The bell meant it was the final lap. Jacob knew he had to push hard to beat the current leading time.

The second set of handlebars used in both road and track time trial events are known as aero bars.

Track cycling races take place in an arena called a velodrome. The track at the Paralympics is usually made of wood.

Not all Para cyclists wear prosthetics when they compete.

Jacob reached the final curve. The finish line was in sight. Jacob leaned his body forward on his bike. He peddled as fast as he could across the finish line. The time to beat was 1:21.30. The clock showed a time of 1:21.16. Jacob had won the race!

Para cycling is a version of the sport for people with different disabilities. Like nondisabled cycling, Para cycling competition includes both track and road events. Athletes must go through a **classification** process to compete. The classifications make sure athletes in each race have similar abilities.

Athletes are given a classification number based on the severity of their **impairment**. The classifications are also separated based on which type of bike an athlete uses. There are four types of bikes in Para cycling. They are traditional bicycle, tricycle, handcycle, and tandem bike.

Track and road cycling each include multiple events. Track cycling races are shorter and test athletes' **agility**. Competition is held indoors on a curved track. In track cycling, athletes typically race against their opponents' times one by one. They do this in events such as the time trial, tandem sprint, and team sprint. There is also an event known as the individual pursuit. This is where two cyclists start on opposite sides of the track. The goal is to catch up to the other cyclist. Whoever successfully catches the other competitor wins the race.

In comparison, road cycling focuses on **endurance**. Cyclists typically race alongside one another over a longer distance in the road race. The first one to cross the finish line wins. There is also a road time trial. It is a race where cyclists compete against the clock. Each athlete starts alone in this event. Road cycling competitions are held outside.

Handcycles and tricycles are only used in road events, while traditional and tandem bikes are used in both road and track events.

PARA CYCLING BIKES AND CLASSIFICATIONS

Traditional bike: C1–C5

Tandem bike: B

Handcycle: H1–H5

Tricycle: T1–T2

CHAPTER TWO

CYCLING FOR ALL

Bicycles have been used as transportation since they were invented in the early 1860s. But people with disabilities did not always have equal access. Bicycles at the time were not made for people with amputations or other conditions.

In 1949, Sir Ludwig Guttmann developed a version of the bike called a bed cycle. The German doctor took his invention to the Stoke Mandeville veterans' hospital in England. Patients with leg amputations were able to exercise without leaving their beds. This helped them gain enough strength in their arms to eventually use a wheelchair.

Modifications to bikes continued to be made in the following years. But most cyclists with disabilities were still competing against nondisabled cyclists. Para cycling competitions began in the 1980s. The first races were for athletes with visual impairments. They rode tandem bicycles.

Road cyclists compete in all kinds of weather, including rain or extreme hot and cold temperatures.

The back part of track cycling helmets is longer than it is on normal bike helmets. This helps athletes be more aerodynamic.

In 1984, cycling events were added to the Paralympic Games. This provided an opportunity for cyclists with disabilities to compete against one another. A total of 22 cyclists competed in seven road events. These athletes all had cerebral palsy. This is a disorder that affects a person's balance and ability to move. At the 1996 Games in Atlanta, Georgia, track cycling events were added to the program. That same year, more classes for people with different disabilities were added. Handcycling became an official event at the 2004 Paralympics in Athens, Greece.

Since the early 2000s, Great Britain has been the most dominant country in Para cycling. But other countries continue to improve. At the 2016 Paralympics in Rio de Janeiro, Brazil, 230 athletes competed in both road and track events. They came from 45 different countries. Out of those 45 countries, 23 came away with at least one Para cycling medal.

INCLUSION
Only two of the 22 cyclists who competed at the 1984 Paralympics were women. No women competed in Para cycling at the 1988 Games in Seoul, South Korea. But as Para cycling evolved, so did its inclusion of female athletes. At the 2016 Rio Games, over 200 cyclists competed. More than 30 percent of those cyclists were women.

The four types of Para cycling bikes each offer modifications to help athletes compete. Parts of a traditional bike can be changed for cyclists with an amputation. Athletes with visual impairments use tandem bikes. Each tandem bike has two seats, two sets of handlebars, and two sets of pedals. A visually impaired rider sits behind someone with full vision. The rider with full vision acts as a guide. They are known as the pilot. The athlete with a visual impairment is known as the stoker. They do most of the pedaling.

Athletes with cerebral palsy or other **neurological** conditions use a tricycle to compete. The third wheel on tricycles helps athletes stay balanced. Handcycles are for athletes with a restriction either in their legs or in both their upper and lower limbs. Athletes use their upper bodies to drive themselves forward. Instead of racing shoes, hand cyclists use hand grips that clip to the pedals. This classification is only for road cycling events.

Modifications can be made to traditional bikes so special prosthetics can be attached to them. This helps athletes with amputations to safely compete.

15

CHAPTER THREE

PARA CYCLING STARS

Great Britain's Sarah Storey was born without function in her left hand. At age ten, she joined her first swim team. Her coach told her that she had started training too late to become a high-level athlete. That only motivated Storey.

From 1992 to 2004, Storey competed as a swimmer in four Paralympic Games. But in 2005, repeated ear infections kept her out of the pool. Storey decided to try Para cycling to stay in shape. She began competing in both road and track events. By the end of 2005, Storey had broken the world record in the 3-kilometer individual pursuit C5.

Strong performances on a traditional bike earned Storey a spot at the 2008 Games in Beijing, China. She went on to win two gold medals. At the Paralympics in Tokyo, Japan, in 2021, Storey won her seventeenth gold medal. That made her Great Britain's most successful Paralympian of all time.

Sarah Storey competes in the women's road race C4–5 at the 2012 Paralympics in London, England. She won four gold medals at those Games.

Like Storey, Great Britain's Neil Fachie originally trained in a different sport. Fachie was born without full vision. But he did not find sports until later in his life. Fachie was studying physics at Aberdeen University when he found his passion for running. He had never trained to be a high-level athlete before. After years of training, Fachie qualified for the 2008 Beijing Games.

After Beijing, Fachie switched to cycling. The strength that he developed through his sprint training impressed Great Britain's cycling coaches. And it was through the national team that Fachie found his tandem guide. Sarah Storey's husband Barney grew close with Fachie. Together they won a gold and silver medal at the 2012 London Games. They also broke the world record in the 1-kilometer time trial B.

Later, Fachie began competing with other guides. Even with new guides, Fachie continued to find success. At the Tokyo Games in 2021, he earned his second career gold medal in the 1-kilometer time trial.

Neil Fachie (left) competes in the men's 1-kilometer time trial B final at the 2012 London Games with his guide Barney Storey. Fachie's winning time set a world record.

Oksana Masters grew up in Ukrainian orphanages. She eventually was adopted by her American mother in 1997. Masters was born with several medical conditions. Upon arriving in the United States, she had both legs amputated above the knee. As a teenager, her mother convinced her to try rowing. Masters won her first Paralympic medal at the 2012 London Games. Coaches from other sports took notice. The US Para Nordic skiing team invited her to try skiing. Masters won two medals at the 2014 Winter Paralympics.

Afterward, Masters suffered a back injury. She decided to try handcycling to stay in shape. Before long she was a Paralympian in that sport, too. Masters finished just off the podium in both road events at the 2016 Rio Games. But she broke through at the Tokyo Games in 2021. Masters won gold medals in both the time trial and road race. A few months later at the Beijing Winter Games, she won seven more medals. With 14 skiing medals, she became the most decorated US Winter Paralympian of all time.

MAKING AN IMPACT

A skiing accident **paralyzed** Muffy Davis from the chest down. At 16, her dreams of becoming an Olympic skier ended. However, a new dream soon began. At the 1998 and 2002 Paralympics, Davis competed in alpine skiing. She later switched to Para cycling. Davis went on to earn three gold medals at the London Games in 2012. She wanted to inspire young athletes to follow their dreams.

Oksana Masters competes in the women's road cycling time trail H5 event at the Tokyo Games.

Masters has said that sports became an important way for her to move past what she experienced in the orphanage. Her story and athletic career have inspired many people. Athletes like Masters have shown the importance of having sports available for everyone, no matter their abilities or background.

GLOSSARY

aerodynamic (ayr-oh-dye-NAM-ik) Aerodynamic means when something is moving very easily and quickly. Track cyclists wear longer helmets that help them be more aerodynamic.

agility (uh-JIL-ih-tee) Agility is the ability to move fast and easily. Para track cycling focuses more on agility than Para road cycling does.

amputated (AM-pyoo-tayt-ed) Amputated means that a limb was removed through surgery. American Oksana Masters had her legs amputated below the knee.

classification (klas-uh-fuh-KAY-shun) Classification is a system used to group athletes with similar abilities so they can compete fairly against one another. Athletes are given a classification based on their disability.

endurance (en-DOOR-uhns) Endurance means having the ability to do something difficult for a long time. Athletes need to have more endurance to compete in Para road cycling.

impairment (im-PAYR-ment) An impairment is something that makes a function or ability more difficult to do. Cyclists with a visual impairment compete on a tandem bike with a guide who has full vision.

modifications (mah-duh-fi-KAY-shuns) Modifications are changing something slightly to meet a specific need. Modifications can be made to bikes to help Para cyclists compete.

neurological (noor-oh-LAW-jih-kal) A neurological condition or disorder affects the nervous system. Athletes with neurological conditions can use tricycles to compete in Para cycling.

paralyzed (PAYR-uh-lized) When someone is paralyzed, a part of their body loses feeling and is not able to move. American Muffy Davis became paralyzed after a skiing accident.

prosthetic (pras-THEH-tik) A prosthetic is an artificial body part. Para cyclists may use a prosthetic when they compete.

FAST FACTS

- Para cycling competitions began in the 1980s to help cyclists with visual impairments continue riding.
- In 1984, cycling became a Paralympic sport. Track cycling events were added to the Paralympics in 1996.
- The four types of bikes used in Para cycling are traditional bike (C1–C5), tandem (B), handcycle (H1–H5), and tricycle (T1–T2).
- Para cycling continues to grow as an international sport. Out of the 45 countries that competed at the 2016 Rio Games, 23 came away with a medal.
- Sarah Storey became Great Britain's all-time Paralympic gold medal leader after the Tokyo Games in 2021.
- Great Britain's Neil Fachie broke the world record in the 1-kilometer time trial B at the 2012 London Games.
- American Oksana Masters won her first two Paralympic cycling medals at the Tokyo Games in 2021. Both were gold.

ONE STRIDE FURTHER

- If you were a Para cyclist, would you want to compete in road or track cycling? Why?
- What is one difference you learned about the different types of bikes?
- Why is it important to have sports for people with disabilities?

FIND OUT MORE

IN THE LIBRARY

Alexander, Lori. *A Sporting Chance: How Ludwig Guttmann Created the Paralympic Games.* Boston, MA: Houghton Mifflin Harcourt, 2020.

Herman, Gail. *What Are the Paralympic Games?* New York, NY: Penguin Workshop, 2020.

Mason, Paul. *Paralympic Power.* London, UK: Wayland, 2019.

ON THE WEB

Visit our website for links about Para cycling:
childsworld.com/links

Note to Parents, Caregivers, Teachers, and Librarians: We routinely verify our Web links to make sure they are safe and active sites. So encourage your readers to check them out!

INDEX

Davis, Muffy, 20

Fachie, Neil, 18

Great Britain, 13, 16, 18
Guttmann, Ludwig, 10

handcycle, 8, 9, 13–14, 20

Masters, Oksana, 20–21

road cycling, 7–8, 13–14, 16, 20

Storey, Sarah, 16, 18

tandem bike, 8, 9, 10, 14, 18
track cycling, 4, 7–8, 13, 16
traditional bike, 8, 9, 14, 16
tricycle, 8, 9, 14